MY 1ST BIRTHDAY

_____
NAME

_____
DATE

_____
PLACE

Copyright © 2022 by Artsy Printing Press
All rights reserved. No part of this publication may be reproduced,
distributed, or transmitted in any form or by any means, including
photocopying, recording, or other electronic or mechanical methods,
without the prior written permission of the publisher.

GUESTS

NAME   BIRTHDAY WISHES

Thank you!

GUESTS

NAME

BIRTHDAY WISHES

Thank you!

GUESTS

NAME　　　　　　　　BIRTHDAY WISHES

Thank you!

GUESTS

NAME   BIRTHDAY WISHES

Thank you!

GUESTS

NAME | BIRTHDAY WISHES

Thank you!

GUESTS

NAME   BIRTHDAY WISHES

Thank you!

GUESTS

NAME   BIRTHDAY WISHES

Thank you!

GUESTS

NAME   BIRTHDAY WISHES

Thank you!

GUESTS

NAME · BIRTHDAY WISHES

Thank you!

GUESTS

NAME　　　　　　　BIRTHDAY WISHES

Thank you!

GUESTS

NAME | BIRTHDAY WISHES

Thank you!

GUESTS

NAME   BIRTHDAY WISHES

Thank you!

GUESTS

NAME · BIRTHDAY WISHES

Thank you!

GUESTS

NAME BIRTHDAY WISHES

Thank you!

GUESTS

NAME   **BIRTHDAY WISHES**

Thank you!

GUESTS

NAME　　　　　　　　BIRTHDAY WISHES

Thank you!

GUESTS

NAME   BIRTHDAY WISHES

Thank you!

GUESTS

NAME   BIRTHDAY WISHES

Thank you!

GUESTS

NAME BIRTHDAY WISHES

Thank you!

Guests

NAME   BIRTHDAY WISHES

Thank you!

GUESTS

NAME   BIRTHDAY WISHES

Thank you!

GUESTS

NAME   BIRTHDAY WISHES

Thank you!

GUESTS

NAME   BIRTHDAY WISHES

Thank you!

GUESTS

NAME   BIRTHDAY WISHES

Thank you!

GUESTS

NAME	BIRTHDAY WISHES

Thank you!

GUESTS

NAME   BIRTHDAY WISHES

Thank you!

GUESTS

NAME   BIRTHDAY WISHES

Thank you!

GUESTS

NAME   **BIRTHDAY WISHES**

Thank you!

Guests

NAME   BIRTHDAY WISHES

Thank you!

GUESTS

NAME BIRTHDAY WISHES

Thank you!

GUESTS

NAME   BIRTHDAY WISHES

THANK YOU!

GUESTS

NAME

BIRTHDAY WISHES

Thank you!

GUESTS

NAME   BIRTHDAY WISHES

Thank you!

GUESTS

NAME   BIRTHDAY WISHES

GUESTS

NAME　　　　　　　　BIRTHDAY WISHES

Thank you!

GUESTS

NAME   BIRTHDAY WISHES

Thank You!

GUESTS

NAME | BIRTHDAY WISHES

Thank you!

Guests

NAME   BIRTHDAY WISHES

Thank you!

Guests

NAME　　　　　　　　　BIRTHDAY WISHES

Thank you!

GUESTS

NAME
BIRTHDAY WISHES

Thank you!

GUESTS

NAME BIRTHDAY WISHES

Thank you!

GUESTS

NAME   BIRTHDAY WISHES

Thank you!

GUESTS

NAME	BIRTHDAY WISHES

Thank you!

GUESTS

NAME   **BIRTHDAY WISHES**

Thank you!

GUESTS

NAME　　　　　　　　BIRTHDAY WISHES

Thank you!

GUESTS

NAME BIRTHDAY WISHES

Thank you!

GUESTS

NAME   BIRTHDAY WISHES

Thank you!

GUESTS

NAME   BIRTHDAY WISHES

Thank you!

GUESTS

NAME   BIRTHDAY WISHES

Thank you!

GUESTS

NAME   BIRTHDAY WISHES

Thank you!

GUESTS

NAME   BIRTHDAY WISHES

Thank you!

GUESTS

NAME   **BIRTHDAY WISHES**

Thank You!

Guests

NAME 　　　　　　　**BIRTHDAY WISHES**

Thank you!

GUESTS

NAME   BIRTHDAY WISHES

Thank you!

GUESTS

NAME | BIRTHDAY WISHES

Thank you!

GUESTS

NAME   BIRTHDAY WISHES

Thank you!

GUESTS

NAME   BIRTHDAY WISHES

Thank you!

GUESTS

NAME BIRTHDAY WISHES

Thank you!

GUESTS

NAME   BIRTHDAY WISHES

GUESTS

NAME BIRTHDAY WISHES

Thank you!

GUESTS

NAME　　　　　　　　BIRTHDAY WISHES

Thank you!

GUESTS

NAME   BIRTHDAY WISHES

Thank you!

GUESTS

NAME   BIRTHDAY WISHES

Thank you!

GUESTS

NAME   **BIRTHDAY WISHES**

Thank You!

GUESTS

NAME BIRTHDAY WISHES

Thank you!

GUESTS

NAME BIRTHDAY WISHES

Thank you!

GUESTS

NAME   BIRTHDAY WISHES

GUESTS

NAME   BIRTHDAY WISHES

Thank you!

Guests

NAME BIRTHDAY WISHES

Thank you!

GUESTS

NAME | **BIRTHDAY WISHES**

Thank you!

Guests

NAME   BIRTHDAY WISHES

Thank You!

GUESTS

NAME   BIRTHDAY WISHES

Thank you!

GUESTS

NAME   BIRTHDAY WISHES

Thank you!

GUESTS

NAME   BIRTHDAY WISHES

Thank you!

GUESTS

NAME　　　　　　　　　　BIRTHDAY WISHES

Thank you!

GUESTS

NAME
BIRTHDAY WISHES

Thank you!

GUESTS

NAME   BIRTHDAY WISHES

Thank you!

GUESTS

NAME | BIRTHDAY WISHES

Thank you!

GUESTS

NAME   BIRTHDAY WISHES

Thank you!

GUESTS

NAME   **BIRTHDAY WISHES**

Thank you!

Gift log

GIFT RECEIVED	GIVEN BY

GIFT RECEIVED	GIVEN BY

GIFT RECEIVED	GIVEN BY

GIFT RECEIVED	GIVEN BY

GIFT RECEIVED	GIVEN BY

GIFT RECEIVED	GIVEN BY

GIFT RECEIVED	GIVEN BY

GIFT RECEIVED	GIVEN BY

GIFT RECEIVED	GIVEN BY

GIFT RECEIVED	GIVEN BY

GIFT RECEIVED	GIVEN BY

GIFT RECEIVED	GIVEN BY

GIFT RECEIVED	GIVEN BY

GIFT RECEIVED	GIVEN BY

GIFT RECEIVED	GIVEN BY

GIFT RECEIVED	GIVEN BY

GIFT RECEIVED	GIVEN BY

GIFT RECEIVED	GIVEN BY

PHOTO/MEMORY

PHOTO/MEMORY

PHOTO/MEMORY

Made in the USA
Columbia, SC
19 September 2023

8e987fd2-e280-4a32-921a-59ddc648e87eR01